ACCOUNTANCY

PART-4

:: Author ::

ROBIN N. VORA

(M.COM., B.ED., SLET)

GUJARAT UNIVERSITY RANKER

PUBLISHED BY

The New Era International Publishing House
HQ. At & Po. Chaveli., Ta- Chansma,
Dist- Patan, North Gujarat, India, Asia.

First Publication: 5th FEBRUARY, 2015

Copyright: Author
(c) ROBIN N. VORA

ISBN:- 978-15-08472-71-1

Price: Rs.750/- INDIA
$ 15 OUTSIDE INDIA

PUBLISHED BY

The New Era International Publishing House
HQ. At & Po. Chaveli., Ta- Chansma,
Dist- Patan, North Gujarat, India, Asia.

Dedicated
to
my
Parents

INDEX

CHAPTER – 1
(" PARTNERSHIP ACCOUNTS ")

☐ FORMULAS ☐

1) *For calculate interest on capital :*

Interest on capital =

$$\frac{Opening\ balance\ of\ capital\ \times\ Rate\ of\ interest}{100}$$

NOTE : *when the opening balance of capital is not given then firstly find out the opening balance of capital with the help of following formula :*

Opening balance of capital = Closing balance of capital + Drawings – Profit

2) *For calculate interest on drawings :*

Interest on drawings =

$$\frac{Amount\ of\ drawings\ \times\ Rate\ of\ interest\ \times\ N}{100}$$

NOTE :

❖ *When a partner has withdrawn at the beginning of the every month – N = 78/12*

❖ *When a partner has withdrawn at the middle of the every*

month – N = **72/12**

❖ When a partner has withdrawn at the end of the every month – N = **66/12**

❖ When a partner has withdrawn at the beginning of the every three months – N = **30/12**

❖ When a partner has withdrawn at the middle of the every three months – N = **24/12**

❖ When a partner has withdrawn at the end of the every three months – N = **18/12**

3) For calculate interest on Current Account :

Interest on Current Account =

$$\frac{\text{Opening balance of Current A/c } \times \text{ Rate of interest}}{\textbf{100}}$$

4) For calculate interest on loan :

Interest on loan =

$$\frac{\text{Amount of loan } \times \text{ Rate of interest } \times \textbf{N}}{\textbf{100}}$$

5) For manager's commission (on profit after charging such commission) :

Manager's commission =

$$\frac{\text{Divisible profit } \times \text{ Rate of Commission}}{\textbf{100 + } \text{Rate of Commission}}$$

☐ THEORY SECTION ☐

❖ *Meaning of Partnership:-*

According to partnership Act, 1932 "Partnership is a relationship between persons who have agreed to share the profit of a business which is carried on by them or any of them." Thus, when two or more persons join hands to carry on a legal business with an objective to earn profit, such an arrangement is called partnership.

The persons who have entered into partnership are individually known as "Partners" and collectively as firm.

❖ *Characteristics of Partnership:-*

➢ *Partnership comes into existence by an agreement (contract). Partnership agreement may be written or oral. But written agreement is more desirable.*

➢ *Partnership is started with a motive to earn profit.*

➢ *Partnership firm comes into existence to carry on some legal business.*

➢ *The partnership business carried on by all the partners or any one of them acting for all. Thus each partner is both an agent and a principal of the other partners.*

➢ *In a partnership firm there must be a minimum of two partners and maximum of 10 in case of banking business and 20 in case of any other business.*

➢ *There is no separation of the ownership and management in a partnership firm.*

Partnership deed is an administrative constitution of a partnership firm which contains the provisions relating to the administration of the firm.

❖ *Partnership Deed :*

Partnership comes into existence as a result of agreement among the partners.The agreement can be either oral or written. The Partnership Act does not requirethat the agreement must be in writing. But wherever it is in writing, the document,which contains terms of the agreement iscalled 'Partnership Deed'. It generally contains the details about all the aspects affecting the relationship between thepartners including the objective of business, contribution of capital by each partner, ratio in which the profits and the losses will be shared by the partnersand entitlement of partners to interest on capital, interest on loan etc. The clauses of partnership deed can be altered with the consent of all the partners. The deed should be properly drafted and prepared as per the provisions of the 'Stamp Act' and preferably registered with the Registrar of Firms.

♣ *Provisions Relevant for Accounting*

✗ *Provision as to Capital:-*
The amount of Capital to be contributed by each partners is mentioned in the partnership deed.

✗ *Interest on Capital:-*
Whether to allow interest on capital or not, and if it is to be allowed then at what percentage is mentioned in the partnership deed. If there is no such

provision in partnership deed interest is not allowed to partners on their capital.

× Provision of Drawings:-

       The amount to be withdrawn interest should be charged on the firm is mentioned in the partnership deed.

× Interest on Drawings:-

       The rate at which interest should be charged on the amount of drawings by partners during the year is mentioned in the partnership deed. If provision there is no such provision in the partnership deed. Interest cannot be charged from partners on their drawings.

× Ratio of sharing Profit-loss :-

       The proportion in which the profit or loss of the business is to be distributed among the partners, is mentioned in a partnership deed. If there is no such provision in the agreement, P &L is then distributed in equal proportion according to the Partnership Act.

× About Salary, Bonus, Commission or Remuneration to be paid to a Partner :-

       If some partner is actively participating in the management of the firm, then any salary, bonus, commission or remuneration to be paid to him is mentioned in the partnership deed.

× Provision as to interest on a Loan given by a Partner to the Firm :-

*The Rate at which interest should be allowed on the loan given by a partner to the firm, is mentioned in the partnership deed. If it is not mentioned then interest is to be allowed at a rate of **6 %** p.a. On the loan given by a partner to the firm.*

✕ *About the Calculation of goodwill of the Firm :-*

How to calculate the goodwill of the firm at the time of admission of a partner or retirement of a partner is mentioned in partnership deed.

✕ *About admission and retirement of a Partner :-*

The terms and condition relating to the admission of a partner and retirement of a partner are mentioned in the partnership deed.

✕ *Provision Regarding Dissolution of Firm :-*

The circumstances under which the partnership firm should be dissolved and the procedure to be followed for such dissolution are mentioned in the partnership deed.

❋ *Provision of Partnership Act relating to Accounting Matters of Partnership Firm : (In Short)*

✕ *P & L is to be distributed equally among the partners.*

✕ *No interest is to be paid on capital invested in the firm by a partner.*

✕ *No interest is to be charged on drawings of a partner from the firm.*

✕ *No partner shall be given any salary, bonus, commission or remuneration.*

✕ *Interest at a rate of 6% p.a is to be allowed on a loan given by a partner to the firm.*

✕ *If some partner has incurred any reasonable exp for the firm, he has a right to get reimbursement for the same.*

✳ **Capital Accounts of partners :-**

There are two method to keep capital accounts of partners in a partnership firm :

✕ *Fluctuating (Floating) Capital Account Method*

✕ *Fixed Capital Account Method.*

✓ **Fluctuating (Floating) Capital Account Method:-**

The method of keeping partners capital account, in which the opening balance of the capital account at the beginning of the year and the closing balance at the end of the year are different, is called fluctuating capital account method.

Partner's Capital Account

Date	Particulars	A	B	Date	Particulars	A	B
	To bal b/d (opening Debit of Capital)	...	...		By bal b/d (opening credit balance of capital)	...	...
	To Drawing a/c To interest on drawings	....	....		By cash a/c (additional capital) By interest on capital	....	....

					By salary, bonus, commission or remuneration	....	....
To share in divisible loss	....	....			By interest on loan	....	....
To balance c/f (closing credit balance of capital)	....	....					
					By share in divisible profit	....	....
					By balance c/f (Closing debit balance of capital)	...	...

❊ *Fixed Capital Account Method :*

The method of keeping a partner's capital account in which the opening balance of the year and the closing balance at the end of the year (except additional capital and capital withdrawn) are not different, is called fixed capital account method. In this method, two accounts are prepared to record the transactions of a partner with the firm :

✓ **Partner's Capital Account.**
✓ **Partner's Current Account.**

Partner's Capital Account (As per Fixed Method)

Date	Particulars	A	B	Date	Particulars	A	B
	To balance b/d (opening debit balance)	...	....		By balance b/d (opening credit balance)	...	....
	To Other asset a/c(Capital withdrawn)	...	....		By cash / bank/other asset a/c	...	....
					By Balance c/d(closing credit balance)		
	To Cash Bank	...	...				
	To Balance c/d(closing credit balance)	...	...				

Partner's Current Account

Date	Particulars	A	B	Date	Particulars	A	B
	To balance b/d (Opening Debit balance of Current A/c)	...	....		By balance b/d (Opening credit balance of Current A/c)	...	....
	To interest on Debit balance of Current A/c				By interest on credit balance of Current A/c		
	To Drawing a/c	...	....		By interest on capital	...	....

				By salary, bonus, commission or remuneration	...	....
To interest on drawings	...	....		By interest on partner's loan	...	....
To share in divisible loss	...	....		By share in divisible profit	...	...
To balance c/f (Closing Debit balance of Current A/c)	...	....		By balance c/f (Closing credit balance of Current A/c)	...	...
					...	...

❖ **Difference between Fixed Capital Account Method and Fluctuating Capital Account Method:-**

Point	Fixed Capital Account Method	Fluctuating Capital Account Method
Meaning	The method of keeping partner's capital account, in which the opening balance and the closing balance (except additional capital and withdrawn capital) are not different is called Fixed Capital Account Method.	The method of keeping partner's capital account, in which there is a difference between the opening balance and the closing balance due to partner's other transactions with firm, is called Fluctuating Capital a/c Method.
Accounts	In this method two	In this method only

	accounts are prepared for each partner in the books of the firm (1) Capital a/c (2) Current a/c	*one capital a/c for each partner is prepared in the books of the firm.*
Record of transaction	*In this method, capital and permanent changes in capital are recorded in capital a/c while other transactions are recorded in current a/c.*	*In this method all the transactions of the partners with the firm are recorded in capital a/c.*
Interest on capital	*In this method, as the amount of capital remains the same for every year (if permanent changes are not there), interest on capital remains the same every year.*	*In this method as the amount of capital changes year, interest on capital also changes every year.*
Balance of account	*Fixed Capital account always shows credit balance while current account may have debit balance or credit balance.*	*According to Fluctuating Capital account method, generally there is credit balance of capital account, Sometimes, there may be debit balance of account.*

> **Drawings Accounts of Partners :-**
  Partner's Capital a/c/Current a/c Dr ....
    To Partner's Drawings a/c ....

(being balance of partner's drawings a/c transferred to capital/current a/c)

❋ *Profit and Loss Appropriation Account :-*

In partnership, after preparing profit and loss account profit and loss appropriation account is prepared, in order to show the distribution of P & L among the partners. Profit and loss appropriation account is merely an extension of P & L account. In Profit and loss appropriation account, if debit side is higher than credit side that is known as divisible loss and if credit side is higher than debit side that is known as divisible profit. The balance of this account (divisible loss / divisible profit)is transferred to partner's capital accounts or current accounts.

Specimen of P & L appropriation Account

Particulars	Amount	Particulars	Amount
To Net loss (transferred from P & L account) To interest on partner's capitals	....	By Net profit (transferred from P & L account) By interest on partner's drawings	....
A - .... B -	....	A - .... B -	....
To interest on credit balance of partner's current accounts	....	By interest on debit balance of partner's current accounts	....

To partner's salary bonus, commission, remuneration	....		
To interest on partner's loan	....		
To divisible profit (transferred to partner's capital/current accounts)		By Divisible loss (Transferred to partner's Capital/ current accounts)	
A -		A -	
B -	....	B -	....
	....		....

* **Difference between P & L Account and P & L Appropriation Account:-**

Point	Profit & Loss Account	Profit & Loss Appropriation Account
Meaning	After preparing trading account, the account prepared to find net P & L of the business is called P & L account.	After preparing P & L account, the account prepared to find out record divisible P & L among the partner's is called P & L Appropriation Account.
Prepared by whom?	Sole proprietorship firms and partnership firms P & L account.	Partnership firms prepare P & L appropriation account

		also.
Debit Side	*On debit side of this account administrative exp, financial exp, selling & distribution exp, depreciation & provision and other miscellaneous exp of the business are recorded.*	*On debit side of this account, interest on capital, interest on credit balance of current account, partner's salary, interest on partner's loan etc. are recorded.*
Credit Side	*On credit side of this account different incomes of the business are recorded.*	*On credit side of this account interest on drawings, interest on debit balance of current account are recorded.*
Result of Account	*The result of this account is called Net Profit or Net Loss.*	*The result of this account is called Divisible Profit or Divisible Loss.*
Where to transfer balance?	*The balance of this account is transferred to P & L appropriation account.*	*The balance of this account is transferred to partner's capital accounts or current accounts.*

☐ PRACTICAL SECTION ☐

1) *Ram withdraws* **Rs.600** *on the first day of each month and Ravan withdraws* **Rs.600** *on the last day of each month,* **5%** *interest is charged on withdrawals. Which partner will have*

to pay more interest as compared to other partner and how much?

2) Vermaand Kaul are partners in a firm.Thepartnership agreement provides that interest on drawings should be charged @ 6% p.a. Verma withdrawsRs 2,000 per month starting from April 01, 2008 to March 31, 2009. Kaul withdrew Rs.3,000 per quarter, starting from April 01, 2008. Calculate interest on partner's drawings.

3) Today, Tomorrow and Yesterday are partners sharing profits and losses in the equal proportion. Manager is to be paid 5 % commission of profit, on profit after deducting his commission. Today gets a profit of Rs.200. Calculate manager's commission.

4) The profit of Rs.1,92,000 partnership firm of Jaymin, Chetan and Divyesh has been distributed by mistake in proportion of 3:2:1 instead of distributing in proportion of 3:4:5 What effect should be given to capital accounts to rectify this error.

5) Good, Better and Best are partners sharing profits and losses in proportion of 6:6:2. Good and Better have given guarantee that Best must get at least Rs.35,000 out of profits. If for the year ending on 30/06/08 the profit of the firm is Rs.1,47,000 then how will the profit be distributed among partners?

6) Jaya,Maya and Daya are partners of a firm on 1/01/01. Their capitals were Rs.30,000, Rs.45,000, Rs.90,000 respectively. At the end of the year, after distributing the

*profit, it was found that interest at **9%** p.a on capital was not calculated. Give a journal entry to rectify the error.*

7) *Amount of closing capital of a partner Foram of a firm is **Rs.83,000** after giving effect for drawings of **Rs.17,000** and divisible profit of **Rs.37,000** Calculate interest on capital at **3.5%** p.a.*

8) *Sun, Moon and Star are partners of a firm. The proportion of their capitals is **1:2:3**. Star is to be paid **4.5%** commission on profit after charging his commission. If profit of the firm, for the year ending on **31/12/11** is **Rs.15,675**. What amount should Star get?*

9) *Tal gets two and a half times of Sangit's share, and Lay gets half the share of Sangit. If profit of the firm, at the end of the year, is **Rs.1,50,000**. Find the amount of profit available to each partner.*

10) *A and B are partners sharing profit and loss in the ratio **3:2**. Manager of their firm is getting **5%** commission on net profit after charging such commission, such amount of commission was **Rs.18,986**, but it was found that while finding profit bad debt amount was taken more by **Rs.2,520** and rent **Rs.1,260** is outstanding to be paid was not taken into consideration. After rectification of above errors find manager's commission and share of profit of partner "A".*

11) *Kanu and Manu are partners in a firm sharing profits in the ratio of **7:5**. They admitted Bhanu as a new partner for **1/6**th share. Bhanu would receive **1/24**th his share from Kanu and **1/8**th part from Manu.*

Calculate new profit sharing ratio.

12) *Meena and Leena are partners sharing profit and loss in the ratio 4:1. The profit and loss appropriation account for the year ending on 31/03/12 is as follows.*

Profit & Loss Appropriation Account

Particulars	Amount	Particulars	Amount
To interest on Capital @ 10%:		By P & L A/c (Net Profit)	81,000
Meena : 18,000		By interest on drawings @ 12%	
Leena : 12,000	30,000	Meena : 900	
To salary (Meena)	18,000	Leena : 300	1,200
To interest on Loan (Leena)	600		
To commission to manager	(?)		
To divisible profit	(?)		
	82,200		82,200

Additional :

× *Manager is to be paid 5% commission on net profit after charging such commission.*

× *Meena has withdrawn amount on 1-10-11. While Leena has withdrawn on 1-1-12.*

From above information prepare capital accounts of partners.

13) *Neeta and Savita are partners sharing profit and loss in their capital ratio. On 1-04-08 total capital of the firm was*

Rs.1,00,000 which is in ratio 3:2 respectively between the partners. Their total drawing were of which is in the ratio 2:3. Interest on drawings is also in proportion of drawing Neeta's interest on drawings is Rs.960. Rate of interest on capital is 12%. Savita is to be given 10% commission on net profit, in case if there is loss then salary Rs.800 per month is to be given to her. Before considering the above adjustment profit of the firm for the year is Rs.40,000. Prepare profit and loss appropriation account and find the share of profit or loss of partners.

☐ LATEST EXAMINATION ☐

14) *A partner has withdrawn Rs.1440 at the end of the every month, if interest on drawings is to be charged at 5% p.a calculate interest on drawings.* **(March,2009, March 10 {Half Amount})**

15) *A gets two and a half times of B's share, and C gets ¾ the profit of B. If profit of the firm, at the end of the year, is Rs.3,06,000. Find the amount of profit available to each partner.* (**March, 2011**)

16) *A,B and C are partners of a firm. The proportion of their capitals is 2:2:1. B is to be paid 10% commission on profit after charging his commission. If profit of the firm, for the year ending is Rs.1,65,000. What amount should B get?*

(**March, 2012**)

17) *Manish, Alpa and Kalpana share share profit and loss in the ratio of 5:3:2 after preparing final a/c it was found that interest on drawing is not calculated. Interest on drawing are Rs.500 and Rs.400 and Rs.300 respectively.*

Write down adjustment entry. (*March, 2013*)

18) *Manisha and Alpa are partners sharing profit in the ratio of 3:1 Alpa and Kalpna are partners sharing profit in the ratio of 2:3 Manager gets Rs.6,600 as commission at the rate of 10% on profit. Distribute the profit among the partners after deducting manager's commission.* (*March, 2014*)

...........×××××××××...........

CHAPTER – 2
(" FINAL ACCOUNTS OF PARTNERSHIP ")

▢ FORMULAS ▢

1) *Adjusted purchase = Opening stock + Net Purchase – Closing stock*

2) *Cost of goods sold = Opening stock of goods + Purchase + Purchase Expense – Closing stock of goods*

▢ IMPORTANT POINTS ▢

❋ **In Final Accounts of a Partnership Firm Prepare :**

1. Trading Account

2. Profit and Loss Account

3. Profit and Loss Appropriation Account

4. Capital Account OR Capital and Current Account

5. Balance Sheet

NOTE : For the business concerns like Tuition classes, Beauty Parlous, Commercial Institutions, Consultation concerns, Hospitals, Dispensaries etc. It is not necessary to prepare Trading Account.

❊ *Remember :*

Name of Account	Reason	Result
Trading Account	a) Debit side is higher than credit side	Gross Loss
	b) Credit side is higher than debit side	Gross Profit
Profit & Loss Account	a) Debit side is higher than credit side	Net Loss
	b) Credit side is higher than debit side	Net Profit
P & L Appro. Account	a) Debit side is higher than credit side	Divisible Loss
	b) Credit side is higher than debit side	Divisible Profit

Specimen of Trading Account

Trading Account of ....for the Year Ended............

Particulars	Rs.	Particulars	Rs.
To Opening Stock	....		
Purchase		By Sales	
Less:Pur.Returns	....	Less : Sales Ret.	......
<u>Expenses relating to Purchase</u>		**<u>Goods going out other then sales</u>**	
Wages		By goods Destroyed by fire	......
Carriage inward	....	By goods given as charity	......
Railway freight	....	By goods withdrawn for personal use	......
Octroi	....	Goods distributed as free samples	......
Customs duty	....	Closing stock	......
Lorry Freight	....	Sales of scrap	......
Dock Charges	....		
Clearing charges	....		
Demurrage	....		
Darmayo	....		
Kharajat expenses	....		
Warfage	....		
Mahajan lago	....		
<u>Expenses relating to production</u>			
Productive wages	....		
Royalty	....		
Factory expenses (rent,taxes, power &	....		

fuel, coal,gas)			
Material consumed (oil & Grease)	....		
Depreciation of factory Building, plant & Machine)	....		
To Gross Profit (Trans. to P & L A/c)	....	**By Gross Loss (Trans.to P & L A/c)**	
	....		....

Specimen of Profit and Loss Account

Profit & Loss Account of ....for the Year

Ended...........

Particulars	Rs.	Particulars	Rs.
To Gross Loss (Transferred from Trading A/c)	....	By Gross profit (Transferred from Trading A/c)	....
Format of Stationery Exp.			
Stationery Stock (Opening)		**Incomes (Revenues)**	
+Stationery-printing expenses.........		Rent received	....
		Commission received	....
– Stationery Stock	....	Brokerage received	....

(Closing)			
Selling & Distribution Exp.		Adat received	....
Carriage outward	....	Interest on investment	....
Commission of salesman	....	Interest on loan given	....
Advertisement exp & Packing exp	....	interest on drawings	....
Delivery van exp	....	bad debts returned	....
Financial exp.		profit on sale of assets	....
Interest on capital	....	Sale of scrap	....
Interest on B.O.D or bank loan taken	....	Misc. income etc.	....
Bank charges & bank commission	....	**Format of Discount Received**	
Other Exp. & losses	....	Dis.Rece.	
Donation		Add:DRC (Adj.).........	
Dep. on assets	....	Less:DRC (T/B)	....
Salary and Rent	....		
Insurance Premium	....		
Taxes & Audit fees	....		
Postage Expenses & Electricity exp	....		
Contribution to provident fund	....		
Loss by fire	....		
Receivable Claim	....		
Format of Bad debt			
B.D. (T/B)			
Add:B.D. (Adj.)			
Add:BDR (Adj.).....			

Less :BDR (T/B)...	....		
Format of Discount Allowed			
Dis. Allow.			
Add: DRD (Adj.)...			
Less :DRD (T/B)....	....		
To Net Profit (Trans. to P & L Appro.A/c)	....	**By Net Loss (Trans. to P & L Appro.A/c)**	....
	....		....

Specimen of P & L appropriation Account

Profit & Loss Appropriation of ....for the Year Ended............

Particulars	Amount	Particulars	Amount
To Net loss (transferred from P & L account)	....	By Net profit (transferred from P & L account)	....
To interest on partner's capitals		By interest on partner's drawings	
A -		A -	
B -	....	B -	....
To interest on credit balance of partner's current	....	By interest on debit balance of partner's current	....

	accounts			accounts	
	To partner's salary bonus, commission, remuneration	....			
	To interest on partner's loan	....			
	To divisible profit (transferred to partner's capital/current accounts) A - .... B -	....		By Divisible loss (Transferred to partner's Capital/ current accounts) A - .... B -	....

✳ ***When Fluctuating (Floating) Capital Account Method is given :***

Partner's Capital Account

Date	Particulars	A	B	Date	Particulars	A	B
	To bal b/d (opening Debit of Capital)	...	...		By bal b/d (opening credit balance of capital)	...	...
	To Drawing a/c	....	....		By cash a/c (additional capital)	....	....
	To interest on	....	....		By interest on capital	....	....

Particulars	A	B	Particulars	A	B
drawings			By salary, bonus, commission or remuneration	....	....
To share in divisible loss	....	....	By interest on loan	....	....
To balance c/f (closing credit balance of capital)	....	....	By share in divisible profit	....	....
			By balance c/f (Closing debit balance of capital)	...	...

✳ When Fixed Capital Account Method is Given:

Partner's Capital Account (As per Fixed Method)

Date	Particulars	A	B	Date	Particulars	A	B
	To balance b/d (opening debit balance)	...	....		By balance b/d (opening credit balance)	...	....
	To Other asset a/c (Capital withdrawn)	...	....		By cash / bank/other asset a/c	...	....
	To Cash Bank	...	...		By Balance c/d (closing

				credit bal.)		
To Balance c/d(closing credit balance)	...	...				

Partner's Current Account

Date	Particulars	A	B	Date	Particulars	A	B
	To balance b/d (Opening Debit balance of Current A/c)	...	....		*By balance b/d (Opening credit balance of Current A/c)*	...	....
	To interest on Debit balance of Current A/c				*By interest on credit balance of Current A/c*		
	To Drawing a/c	...	....		*By interest on capital*	...	....
	To interest on drawings	...	....		*By salary, bonus, commission or remuneration*	...	....
	To share in divisible loss	...	....		*By interest on partner's loan*	...	....
	To balance c/f (Closing Debit balance of Current A/c)	...	....		*By share in divisible profit*	...	...
					By balance c/f (Closing credit balance of Current A/c)	...	...
						...	...

Balance Sheet of Shree.........as on........

Liabilities	Rs.	Assets	Rs.
Capital Accounts		**Fixed Assets**	
		Goodwill	....
A :		Land	....
B :	......	Building	....
		Leasehold assets	....
Current Accounts		Machinery	....
(Credit Balance)		Furniture & Fittings	....
		Patent, trademark, copy right	....
A :			
B :	....	Live Stock	....
Reserves		Vehicles	....
general reserve	....	**Investments**	
		Government Securities	....
Capital reserve	....		
		Investment of provident Fund	....
Secured Loans		Investment of Share	....
Loan taken from bank	....	**Current Assets**	
Institutional Loan	....	Dead Stock	....
Unsecured Loans		Closing stock	....
Fixed deposit	....	Debtors(Customers or Dues)	....
Loan taken from friends	....		
Current Liabilities & provision		Stores & Spare parts, Loose tools	....
B.O.D	....	Cash balance	....
Bills payable	....	Bank balance	....
Creditors(Suppliers	....	Income due but not	....

or Debt)		received	
Outstanding Exp	……….	Loan Given	……….
Incomes received in advance	……….	Bills receivable	……….
provision for Tax	……….	Loan given to employee	……….
provident Fund	……….	Advance paid for purchases	……….
		Expenses paid in advance	……….
		Preliminary Expenses	……….
		Discount on Share/ Debenture	……….
		Current Accounts	
		(Debit Balance)	
		A : ……….	
		B : ……….	……….
	……….		……….

⇒ **Important Adjustments : (Give Two Effects)**

No.	Adjustment	Effects
1.	**Closing Stock**	a) Trading A/c credit side b) Balance sheet asset side as an asset
2.	**Outstanding expense**	a) Trading or profit & loss a/c debit side - addition to the exp b) Balance sheet liabilities side as a liability

3.	Prepaid exp	a)Trading or profit & loss a/c debit side - deduction from the exp b)Balance sheet asset side as an asset
4.	Income due but not received	a)P & L a/c credit side - addition to the respective income. b)Balance sheet asset side as an asset
5.	Income received in advance	a)P & L a/c credit side - deduction the respective income. b)Balance sheet liability side as liability.
6.	Interest on capital	a) Profit & loss appropriation a/c debit side b) partner's capital or current a/c credit side
7.	Interest on drawing	a) Profit & loss appropriation a/c credit side b) partner's capital or current a/c debit side
8.	Interest on current a/c (credit balance)	a) Profit & loss appropriation a/c debit side b) partner's current a/c credit side
9.	Interest on current a/c (debit balance)	a) Profit & loss appropriation a/c credit side b) partner's current a/c debit side
10.	Interest on loan	a) Profit & loss a/c debit side b) Balance sheet – liability side
11.	Interest on partner's loan	a) Profit & loss appropriation a/c debit side b) partner's capital or current a/c credit side
12.	Outstanding	a) Profit & loss appropriation a/c debit

	salary, remuneration etc. to Partners	side b) partner's capital or current a/c credit side
13..	Depreciation on assets	a) Profit & loss a/c debit side b) Balance sheet - asset side deducted from respective asset
14.	Bad debts (New/adj.)	a) Profit & loss a/c debit side - In format of Bad debts (+) b) Balance sheet - asset side deducted from debtors
15.	Provision for doubtful debts (B.D.R.) (New)	a) Profit & loss a/c debit side - In format of Bad debts (+) b) Balance sheet - asset side deducted from debtors
16.	Discount reserve on debtors (New)	a) Profit & loss a/c debit side - In format of Discount (+) b) Balance sheet - asset side deducted from debtors
17.	Unrecorded purchase	a)Trading account debit side addition to purchase b)Balance sheet liabilities side as an addition to the creditors
18.	Unrecorded sales	a)Trading a/c credit side addition to sales b) Balance sheet assets side as an addition to the debtors
19.	Goods with-drawn for personal use & the same is	a)Trading a/c credit side as goods withdrawn for personal use b) partner's capital or current a/c debit side

	not recorded	
20.	*Goods destroyed by fire*	a)*Trading a/c credit side as goods given destroyed by fire* b)*P & L a/c debit side as loss due to fire*
21.	*Goods destroyed by fire & insurance company accepts a partial claim*	a) *Trading a/c credit side as goods destroyed by fire* b) *Balance sheet asset side, insurance company as debtors & in P & L a/c loss due to fire as expense*
22.	*Stationery stock*	a)*P & L a/c debit side as deduction from Stationary expenses* b)*Balance sheet asset side as stationery stock*
23.	*Write off proportionate part of lease hold property*	a)*P & L a/c debit side* b)*Balance sheet asset side as deduction from the asset*

No	Adjustment	Effect
1.	**Closing Stock**	Balance sheet asset side as an asset
2.	**Depreciation on assets**	Profit & loss a/c debit side
3.	**Closing Stock of Stationery**	Balance sheet asset side as stationery stock
4.	**Outstanding expense**	Balance sheet liabilities side as a liability
5.	**Income due but not received**	Balance sheet asset side as an asset
6.	**Income received in advance**	Balance sheet liabilities side as a liability
7.	**Prepaid exp**	Balance sheet asset side as an asset
8.	**Depreciation Fund**	Balance sheet - asset side deducted from respective asset
9.	**Provident Fund**	Balance sheet liabilities side as a liability
10.	**Investment of Provident Fund**	Balance sheet asset side as an asset

11.	*Apprentice Premium received in Advance*	*Balance sheet liabilities side as a liability*
12.	*Bad debt Reserve (when bad debt (T/B),Bad debt (Adj.), bad debt Reserve (Adj.)are not given at that time*	*Balance sheet - asset side deducted from debtors*

Other Important Hidden Adjustments which are Given in Trial Balance :

(Give Only One Effect)

NOTE :

> ➢ *BDR : Bad debt reserve*

> ➢ *DRD: Discount reserve on debtors*

> ➢ *DRC: Discount reserve on creditors*

> ➢ *B.O.D : Bank overdraft*

> ➢ *Adj.: Adjustment*

> ➢ *T/B: Trial balance*

$$\boxed{\text{❒ PRACTICAL SECTION ❒}}$$

1. *From the trial balance as on **30/06/12** and adjustments, prepare final accounts of partnership firm of Patel and Shah.*
Trail Balance as on 30/06/2012

Particular	J.F.	Debit Rs.	Credit Rs.
Capital and Drawings :			
Patel :		6,500	2,27,500
Shah :		9,750	1,62,500
Furniture and fixtures		1,46,250	–
Salary		4,87,500	–
Typewriter's machines		97,500	–
Trading exp.		9,750	–
Rent and taxes		29,250	–
Bank		52,000	–
Tuition fees		–	6,01,250
Telegram and postage		6,500	–
Outstanding Tuition fees		16,250	–
Cash		13,000	–
Misc.exp.		32,500	–
Printing and stationary		81,250	–
Creditors		–	82,550
10 % loan of Palav		–	97,500
Building		1,62,500	–
Electricity charges		19,500	–

Repairing		9,750	–
Bank interest		–	6,500
Discount received		–	5,200
Bad debts recovered		–	13,000
Stationary stock (30-06-2012)		16,250	–
		11,96,000	11,96,000

Adjustments :

(1) Calculate interest 10% on the capital, 12 % on the drawings.

(2) Provide a depreciation 5% on the building and 10% on the typewriter's machines.

(3) A salary of Rs.32,500 is unpaid. And a note of is Rs.100 found to be duplicate.

(4) Patel is entitled to receive 10% commission on the divisible profit.

(5) Shah is to be paid a monthly remuneration Rs.5000.

(6) On 1-10-09 Patel has introduced additional capital of Rs.65,000.

2. From the Trial Balance as on 31/03/12 and adjustments, prepare final accounts of partnership firm of Laxmi and Sarasvati.

The Trial Balance as on 31/03/12

Debit Balance	Amount Rs.	Credit Balance	Amount Rs.
Opening stock	75,000	Capital :	
Purchase	10,00,000	Laxmi	1,25,000
Debtors	3,75,000	Sarasvati	1,25,000

Bank balance	30,000	Traders	1,25,000
Carriage inward	45,000	Sales	15,00,000
Electricity exp.	5,000	Bills payable	12,500
Insurance Premium	20,000	Provident fund	18,750
Salary	1,05,000	Bank overdraft	15,000
Rent & Taxes	7,500	Outstanding salary	10,000
Carriage outward	52,500		
Receivable claim	12,500		
Advertisement suspense A/c	22,500		
Furniture & fittings (Cost price Rs.80,000)	57,500		
Bills receivable	15,000		
Office equipments (Cost price Rs.60,000)	25,000		
Bad debts	10,000		
10% Investment (1-1-12)	15,000		
Wages	37,500		
Investment of P.F.	18,750		
Prepaid insurance	2,500		
	19,31,250		19,31,250

Adjustments :

(1) The closing stock was **Rs.2,62,500.**

(2) In reference to receivable claim, it was settled for Rs.5,000 with Insurance Company.

(3) From advertisement suspense a/c, write off 50% as advertisement expenses of the current year.

(4) Calculate 5% depreciation on Furniture & fittings as per straight line method and 10% depreciation on office equipments as per diminishing method.

(5) A bill of Rs.5,000 that was received from customers and discounted in the bank and is dishonored on 31-03-12.

(6) Provide 2% BDR on customers.

3. Kaju, Badam, and Pista are partners of a partnership firm. Prepare the final accounts from the trial balance as on 30/06/11 and adjustments.

Trial Balance as on 30/06/11 of a partnership firm of Kaju, Badam, and Pista

Debit Balance	Amount	Credit Balance	Amount
Capital :		Capital :	
Pista	24,000	Kaju	2,40,000
Drawings : Kaju	24,000	Badam	2,40,000
: Badam	24,000	Sales	6,00,000
: Pista	12,000	Purchase return	4,800
Stock (Date:1-7-10)	1,20,000	Payable	27,200
Purchases	2,40,000	Interest	2,880
Sales return	7,200	Discount	4,320
Salary	48,000	B.D. reserve	4,800
Mahajan Lago	48,000		
Furniture	10,560		
Carriage inward	12,000		
Trading expenses	28,800		

Receivables	1,44,000		
Factory rent	6,000		
Bank balance	58,640		
Discount	5,280		
Building	1,44,000		
Advance Income tax	480		
Bills receivable	4,800		
Dep. on furniture	1,440		
Lease hold property	48,000		
Loose Tools	48,000		
Travelling Expenses	14,400		
Taxes and insurance	2,400		
Mortgage Loan	48,000		
	11,24,000		**11,24,000**

Adjustments :

1) Closing stock was **Rs.1,80,000** and calculate **5%** interest on capital.

2) From the divisible profit Pista is entitled to receive **Rs.4,800** before distribution of it. Subsequently the remaining profit is distribute in the proportion of **2:2:1**.

3) The manager of the firm is allowed **10%** commission on the profit after deduction of such commission.

4) Provide a depreciation **5%** on the machines and **10%** on the loose tools.

5) A salary **Rs.4,800** is prepaid and bad debts reserve is to be increased by **Rs.9,600**.

6) *From bills receivable one bill of* **Rs.1,200** *is found to be irrecoverable.*

4. *Shubh and Labh are partners of a partnership firm. They distribute the profit in the proportion of* **6:4.** *From the following Trial Balance as on* **31-03-09** *and adjustments, prepare the final accounts of the firm.*

Trial Balance Sheet as on **31-3-09**

Particular	J.F.	Debit Rs.	Credit Rs.
Net profit		–	75,000
Capital – Drawings : Shubh		4,500	37,500
: Labh		6,000	62,500
Current Accounts : Shubh		11,500	–
: Labh		–	6,000
Salary : Shubh		9,000	–
Cash and Bank		30,000	500
Customers and Traders		27,500	9,000
P.F. and Investment of P.F.		6,000	9,500
Outstanding wages		–	1,500
Insurance Premium paid in advance		4,000	–
Furniture		18,000	–
Shares – Investments		12,500	–
Investment Fluctuation fund		–	3,000
Closing stock (Date :31-3-09)		12,000	–
Leasehold building		30,000	–
Outstanding rent		4,000	–
Commission received in advance		–	2,500

Shubh's loan (From:*1-6-2008*)		–	15,000
Interest on Shubh's loan		500	–
Machines		45,000	–
		2,20,500	2,22,000

⇒*Additional Information :*

1. *Calculate interest @10% on the capital, @ 5% on the drawings and @ 10% on the balance of current accounts.*

2. *A monthly salary of Rs.1,000 is payable to Shubh.*

3. *A bill of Rs.2,000 was received, which is not recorded in the books.*

4. *On 31-03-2009 Labh has brought personal furniture of Rs.2,000, which is not recorded in the books.*

5. *Shubh is entitled to receive 10% commission on the profit after giving the treatment of the above mentioned adjustments.*

5. *Ganga and Jamna are partners of a firm. From the following trial balance as on 31-3-10 and additional details prepare profit-loss A/c P & L A/c App. A/c partner's Capital Account And a Balance Sheet of the Firm.*

Trial Balance as on 31- 3- 10

Debit Balances	Amount	Credit Balances	Amount
Drawings :		Capital :	
Ganga	4,800	Ganga	24,000
Jamna	3,200	Jamna	16,000
Adjusted	1,06,000	Sales	2,00,000

Purchase Goods Stock (31-3-10)	28,000	Suppliers	30,000
Customers	48,000	Goods distributed as sample	2,000
Wages-Salary	10,000	BOD	14,000
Trading Exp	16,000		
Building	50,000		
Furniture & Fittings	10,000		
Office Equipments	4,000		
Stock of packing Materials	4,000		
Cash Balance	2,000		
	2,86,000		2,86,000

❖ *Adjustments :*

1) *Calculate 8 % interest on capital and 12 % interest on drawings. Ganga has withdrawn Rs.400 at the end of every month and Jamna has withdrawn on 1-10-09.*

2) *A credit sales of Rs. 10,000 is to be recorded, the total of sales book is overcast by Rs.2,000.*

3) *Provide for additional bad debts of Rs. 2,000 and provide 5 % for bad debts reserve.*

4) *The fittings of Rs. 4,000 became obsolete for this accounting treatment is not given.*

5) *On Failure of supply of goods to a customer, the court has approved a claim for Rs.4,000.*

6) *Rs.2,000 as outstanding wages is recorded in wages account, but not recorded in outstanding wages account.*

6. *Pen and Pencil are partners of a firm. From the following trial balance and adjustments, prepare Profit – Loss a/c P & L A/c Appropriation A/c Current Accounts and Balance Sheet*

Trial Balance as on 31- 3- 11

Accounts	L.F	Debit	Credit
Capital Accounts :			
Pen		–	20,000
Pencil		–	20,000
Current Accounts :			
Pen (1-7-10)		4,000	–
Pencil (1-10-10)		–	5,000
Interest on Capital :			
Pen		500	–
Pencil		–	750
Interest on Current Accounts :			
Pen		200	–
Pencil		–	100
Drawings Accounts :			
Pen (1-1-11)		1,000	–
Pencil (1-10-10)		1,000	–
Interest on Drawings :			
Pen		–	10
Pencil		–	20
Office Machinery (old) (1-4-10)		10,000	–
Office Machinery (New) (1-1-11)		4,000	–
Apprentice Premium		–	2,400

Pencil's loan and its interest (1-10-09)	100	5,000
Office salary	20,000	–
Rent	–	10,000
Salary of Pen (**Per month Rs 1,000)**	10,000	–
Creditors	–	5,000
Insurance-premium	1,800	
BOD	–	15,000
Trading A/c and Bad debts Return	10,000	820
Debtors	10,000	–
Stock of Goods (31-3-11)	10,000	–
Total	**83,350**	**83,350**

❖ *Adjustments :*

1) Calculate **10 %** depreciation on old and new machinery of office.

2) Calculate **5 %** interest on capital and **6 %** interest on drawings as well as current accounts.

3) Apprentice premium is received for **12** months from **1-4-10**

4) Office salary is to be paid **Rs. 1,500** per month.

5) Included in insurance premium is an amount of **Rs. 1,200** which is paid for the year ending on **30-9-11**.

6) Rent is received upto **31-1-11.**

7. Dr. Ritu and Dr. Nitu run Mahavir Arogya Niketan Hospital in Partnership. Prepare the final accounts from the Trial Balance as on **31/03/2012** and adjustments.

Trail Balance as on 31/03/2012

Particular	J.F.	Debit	Credit
Capital and Drawings : *Ritu*		*27,000*	*2,25,000*
: Nitu		*18,000*	*1,50,000*
Fees received from patients			
Indoor patient's fees		–	*3,00,000*
Outdoor patient's fees		–	*1,50,000*
X-Ray fee		–	*1,35,000*
Visit fee		–	*75,000*
Laboratory fee		–	*90,000*
Medicines :			
Opening stock		*37,500*	–
Purchase during the year		*1,05,000*	–
Staff salary		*67,500*	–
X-Ray Machine		*3,00,000*	–
Electricity charges		*55,500*	–
Taxes (Hospital)		*7,500*	–
Sundry expenses		*30,000*	–
Medical equipments		*75,000*	–
Furniture		*60,000*	–
Motor car		*1,20,000*	–
Repairing of medical equipments		*15,000*	–
Building		*2,25,000*	–
Fees receivable from patients		*45,000*	–
Creditors		–	*90,000*
Cash Balance		*4,500*	–
Bank Balance		*22,500*	–
		12,15,000	*12,15,000*

Adjustments :

✓ Partners distribute half the profit in **3:3** proportion and the remaining in the proportion of their capital.

✓ A fees of **Rs. 78,000** is yet to be received.

✓ Closing sock at the end of the year for medicine was of **Rs.30,000.**

✓ The purchase of medicine during the year **Rs.7,500** which was not recorded in the books, but it was included in the closing stock.

✓ Partners are entitled to receive **10%** interest on capital and charge **10%** interest on the drawings on an average of **6** months.

✓ Provide a depreciation at **5%** on building and **10%** on the furniture.

8. Actor and Actress are partners in a partnership firm. From the trial balance of **31-12-11** and other information prepare final accounts of their partnership firm.

Trial Balance Sheet as on *31-12-11*

Particular	J.F.	Debit	Credit
Capital – Drawings : Actor		18,000	1,80,000
: Actress		24,000	2,70,000
Current Accounts : Actor		18,000	–
: Actress		–	6,000
Goods stock (*1-4-08*)		1,04,484	–
Cash and Bank		3,150	29,892
Salary		30,000	–

Sales – Purchase		3,30,117	5,76,096
Machinery		1,84,464	–
Depreciation on Machinery		20,496	–
Goods return		10,626	18,219
Mahajan lago		7,956	–
Customers and Traders		72,000	25,200
Bills		1,12,224	59,400
Rent (upto 30-11-01)		27,786	–
Furniture		1,26,900	–
Sales of Furniture (1-7-2001)		–	15000
Insurance premium (Including Rs.5,400 for the year ending on 31-03-02)		8550	–
Brokerage		–	5220
Bad debts and bad debts return		1500	3090
Other expenses		17850	–
Travelling exp.		951	–
Actor's loan (From: 1-7-01)		–	24900
Discount		945	1281
Trading exp.		1599	–
Advertisement exp.		15,000	–
Machines (addition of Rs.18,000 on 30-9-01)		78,000	–
		12,14,598	12,14,298

Additional Information:

➢ *Calculate interest **10%** on the capital, **12%** on the drawings and **9%** on the balance of current accounts.*

➢ *Calculate **9%** depreciation on Machinery and **5%** on furniture.*

➢ *Actor is to be paid **Rs.1,050** as a monthly salary, out of which the salary of **4** months is withdrawn and included in payment of salary.*

➢ ***75%*** *brokerage is received in advance.*

➢ *On **31-10-2001** Actress has introduced additional capital of **Rs.30,000**. Actor has withdrawn **Rs.1,500** at the end of the every month, while Actress has made a drawing on **30-6-2001**.*

➢ *Actress has withdrawn goods worth **Rs.3,000** on **31-10-2001**, which is recorded in the sales at **Rs.3,600**.*

➢ *Divisible profit upto **Rs.60,000** is to be distributed in equal proportion while the remaining in the proportion of the capital.*

➢ *On receipt of change of **Rs.1,000** note, a note of is **Rs.100** found to be duplicate.*

➢ *A debtor of **Rs.3,600** was declared insolvent and **40** paise dividend per rupee is expected.*

> *Closing stock is of **Rs.74,100**. Details relating to price are as under.*

> *Market price is - **Rs.30,300**   cost price is - **Rs.31,500***

> *Market price is - **Rs.35,000**   cost price is - **Rs.33,600***

> *When remaining stock requires repairs **25%**.*

9. *P and R are partners in a partnership firm. From the trial balance of **31-12-10** and other information prepare final accounts of their partnership firm.*

The trial balance of 31-12-10

Debit Balances	Rs.	Credit Balances	Rs.
Drawings : P	12,000	Capital : P	33,000
R	12,000	R	38,400
Purchases	1,04,000	Sales	1,84,000
Goods return	1,600	Goods return	1,200
Stock of goods (1-01-10)	16,000	Provision for bad debts	2,000
Salaries	18,000	Bank loan	13,500
Office expenses	9,000	Traders	40,000
Carriage inward	3,000	Bills Payable	1,800
Carriage outward	4,500	General reserve	8,000
Bad debts	1,400	Loan acquired	4,000
Customers	67,000	Brokerage	1,600
Bills receivable	2,000		

Cash and Bank	5,600		
Investments	14,000		
Machines	24,000		
Lease-hold building (From **1-01-10** for **5** years)	30,000		
Insurance premium (Including Rs.**2,400** for the year ending on **31-03-11)**	3,400		
	3,27,500		**3,27,500**

Adjustments :

a) Closing stock was **Rs.28,600** ,out of which the market value of **10%** goods is **20%** less.

b) Investments are valued at **Rs.12,000.**

c) ¾ Brokerage is received in advance.

d) Unpaid salary **Rs.2,000.**

e) Write off **Rs.1,000** as bad debts from debtors and make a provision for bad debts reserve at **5%.**

(March,09)

10. CD and DVD run a music training institute in partnership. They distribute half the profit equally and the remaining in the proportion of their capital. From the following Trial Balance as on **31-03-09** and adjustments, prepare the final accounts of the firm.

Adjustments:

❖ Training Fees outstanding of **Rs.2,00,800.**

Particular	J.F.	Debit Rs.	Credit Rs.
Capital and Drawings : CD		1,20,000	7,00,000
: DVD		1,00,000	3,00,000
Musical instruments		20,00,000	–
Instruments' rent		–	45,000
Instruments' repairing		25,000	–
Cash and Bank Balance		2,15,000	–
Salary		2,50,000	–
Rent		1,00,000	–
Sundry expenses		20,000	–
Furniture and Creditors		50,000	4,50,000
Training Fees		–	10,00,000
Taxes		30,000	–
Investment in TCS and its dividend		3,00,000	55,000
Stationary		30,000	–
Insurance Premium		10,000	–
Loan of SBI		–	7,00,000
		32,50,000	32,50,000

❖ Provide **10%** depreciation on Musical instruments.
❖ **10%** interest on SBI loan is outstanding.

❖   *Partners are entitled to get* **5%** *interest on capital. Calculate* **8%** *interest on drawings. CD has withdrawn an equal amount every month at the beginning of every month. DVD has withdrawn on* **1-10-08.**

❖   *CD is to be paid* **5%** *commission on the net profit after deducting such commission.* **(March,10)**

11.   *The Annual Accounts of partnership firm of Dave and Patel are as follows.*

Trading and Profit and loss account for the year ended 31-3-10 of partnership firm of Dave and Patel

Particulars	Rs.	Particulars	Rs.
To Cost of goods sold	4,64,000	By Sales	7,84,000
To Office expenses	80,000	By Incomes	8,000
To Sales expenses	64,000		
To Financial expenses	16,000		
To Sundry expenses	16,000		
To Net Profit (Transferred to capital a/c)			
Dave : **91,200**			
Patel : <u>**60,800**</u>	1,52,000		
	7,92,000		7,92,000

Balance sheet as on *31-03-10*

Liabilities	Rs.	Assets	Rs.
Capital :		Current assets (Including Debtors)	1,12,000
Dave : 1,60,000		Investments	48,000
+ Net Profit : <u>91,200</u>		Fixed assets	2,40,000
2,51,200			
– Drawings : <u>48,000</u>	2,03,000		
Patel : 1,20,000			
+ Net Profit : <u>60,800</u>			
1,80,800			
– Drawings : <u>24,000</u>	1,56,800		
Liabilities :	32,000		
Suspense account	8,000		
	4,00,000		4,00,000

After the preparation of the Final Accounts it was traced out that :

1) The interest on the capital is computed at **5%**.
2) Provide **10%** depreciation on the Fixed Assets.
3) Prepaid rent **Rs. 800**.
4) The interest of **Rs.1,600** is yet to be received on the investments.
5) Provide bad debts reserve of **Rs.2,400**
6) The total of sales book is under cast by **Rs.8,000**.
7) Unrecorded credit purchase is **Rs.3,200.(March'11)**

12. Trail Balance is as under of Monan and Kanan's partnership firm. From the trial balance of **31-03-09** and other information prepare final accounts of their partnership firm.

Particular	J.F.	Debit Rs.	Credit Rs.
Capital – Drawings : Manan		3,000	2,80,000
: Kanan		4,500	2,20,000
Sales - Purchase		80,000	1,20,000
Advertisement exp.		7,000	–
Machinery (office)		1,50,000	–
Outward carting charge		850	–
Traders and Customers		25,000	35,000
Building		2,50,000	–
Wages – not paid & wages		750	2,600
Commission paid in advanced		350	–
Purchase of office Machinery (1-10-08)		40,000	–
Trading exp.		1,300	–
8% Central Government loan		30,000	–
Goods stock (1-4-08)		42,000	–
Goods return		16,000	14,000
Customs duty		1,300	–
Manan's loan		–	10,000
Tolai		450	–
Office salary		15,000	–
Interest on loan		400	–
Bank A/c and cash A/c		20,700	3,000

Current Accounts	: Manan		8,000	–
	: Kanan		–	12,000
			6,96,600	6,96,600

Adjustments :

1) Closing stock is **Rs.80,000**.
2) Calculate **10%** depreciation on Machinery and Building.
3) A debtor of **Rs.10,000** was declared insolvent and liquidator was given instruction that firm will get only **50%** of final dividend. Provide **5%** B.D.R.
4) Interest on bank A/c of **Rs.300** is not recorded.
5) The goods of **Rs.2,000** was unrecorded in sales return book.. **(March'12)**

13. Priti and Dipak are partners of a partnership firm, prepare the final accounts of the firm :

Trial Balance Sheet as on 31-3-2009

Liabilities	Rs.	Assets	Rs.
Capital		**Capital**	
Priti 1-10-08	5,000	Priti	20,000
Dipak 1-1-09	10,000	Dipak	30,000
		Current A/c of	
Current A/c Priti	6,000	Dipak	4,000
Interest on capital		Int. on Drawing	
Priti	700	Priti	100
Dipak	1,000	Dipak	50
		Priti's Loan	
Machinery	40,000	(1-10-08)	10,000

Int. on loan	200	Rent	12,000
Salary (every month) 1000	13,000	Creditors	5,000
Dipak's Salary	5,500	Trading A/c	24,700
Debtors	15,000	Suspense A/c	300
Outstanding rent	2,000	Bank Overdraft	5,450
Bad debts	1,300	Int. on current A/c Priti	100
Closing stock (including Rs.1,200 for the year ending on 30-06-09)	10,000

2,000 | Insurance premium | |
| | 1,11,700 | | 1,11,700 |

Adjustments :

1) Calculate 5 % interest on capital 6% on drawing and 10 % on balance of current A/c.

2) Provide for depreciation @ 10 % on machines.

3) Dipak is to be paid Rs.500 as a monthly salary.

4) The total of sales book is under cast by Rs.300.

5) Out of the net profit Rs.1,700 is to be transferred to general reserve. (March'13)

14. *Naram and Garam are partners of a firm distributing profits and loss in the proportion of their capital.*

Balance Sheet as on 31-12-2009

Liabilities	Rs.	Assets	Rs.
Drawing :		**Capital :**	
Naram	7,500	Naram	1,40,000
Garam	5,000	Garam	1,20,000
Opening stock	15,000	Sales	1,20,000
Purchases	80,000	Purchase returns	2,000
		Creditors	
Sales Return	3,000	**(Payable)**	79,000
		Outstanding	
Debts (receivable)	27,400	wages	700
Salaries			
(Upto 28-2-08)	13,200	Naram's loan	30,000
		Discount	
Machines	71,760	received	6,600
Dep. on machines	6,240	Bank overdraft	2,800
		Garam's current	
Building	80,000	a/c	14,000
Wages	1,600		
Insu. Premium	1,800		
Discount Allowed	3,200		
Int. on loan	1,200		
Furniture	87,000		
Stationery exp.	7,000		
Advertisement exp.	36,000		
Cash balance	51,200		
Naram's current A/c	17,000		
	5,15,100		5,15,100

❖ *Adjustments :*

1) The closing stock is **Rs.21,000** *including stationery stock* **Rs.2,000.**

2) Increase the rate of deprecation on machines at **10 %.**

3) ¼ of advertisement expenses is to be carried forward to the next year.

Prepare the final accounts. **(March'14)**

.............××××××××××.............

CHAPTER – 3
(" RECONSTRUCTION OF PARTNERSHIP ")

☐ FORMULAS ☐

1) *Sacrificing ratio = The old share of profit of partner – The new share of profit of partner.*

   While calculating sacrificing ratio, if the answer is negative (–), then it is a benefit (Gain) to the partner and not sacrifice.

2) *Gaining ratio = New share of profit – Old share of profit*

   *If answer is **negative (–)** then it is a sacrifice and not a gain.*

☐ IMPORTANT POINTS ☐

⇒ *If the **assets values are increased** and **liabilities values are decreased** then the difference of the amount is to be **credited to the Revaluation Account**.*

⇒ *If the **assets values are decreased** and **liabilities values are increased** then the difference of the amount is to be **debited to the Revaluation Account**.*

☐ THEORY SECTION ☐

The reasons may be as follows " Reconstruction of Partnership". Changes in Partnership due to several reasons.

> *The change in the ratio of Profit and loss sharing or allocation between continuing partners.*
> *Admission of a new partner in exiting partnership firm.*
> *Retirement or death of a partner of exiting partnership firm.*

The changes in P & L sharing or distribution Ratio Between Continuing Partners:-

Generally when there is a change in profit-sharing ratio of existing partner, then some partners have to sacrifice certain portion of their profit which will be the gain for the other partner. So at the time of reconstruction of partnership, two important points are to be noted:

(1) Sacrificing ratio.
(2) Gaining ratio.

(1) Sacrificing ratio:-

At the time of change in the ratio of P &L if there is a change in profit sharing ratio of partners, a portion of profit of certain partners is reduced, they get less share as compared to what they used to get before the changes in their profit sharing ratio. This reduced the share of profit of a partners is called **"Sacrificing ratio"**.

Sacrificing ratio of partner = The old share of profit of partner – The new share of profit of partner.

While calculating sacrificing ratio, if the answer is negative (−) , then it is a benefit to the partner and not sacrifice. Gain = **new profit sharing ratio – old profit sharing ratio.**

(2) Gaining Ratio :

When there is a change in profit and loss sharing ratio of partners, their share of profit of some partners reduces and other partners' Share of profit increases. So, some partners' share of profit is higher than the prior one. This higher share of profit of partners is called " **Gaining ratio**".*

Gaining ratio = New share of profit – Old share of profit

If answer is **negative (-) then it is a sacrifice and not a gain.**

✳ **Revaluation Accounts of Asset and Liabilities of Partnership Firm :-**

The book value of asset and liabilities recorded in books of partnership firm may be higher or lesser than its market or real value. It may be possible that, with the passage of time, the price of fixed assets such as land and building may go up. In the same manner, there may not be any provision for reserve on Debtor or bills receivable. Due to all these reasons if partners have decided to revaluate the assets and liabilities of the firm, then "**Revaluation Accounts**" *is opened to record the effects for these revaluations. This Account is also known as* "*P & L Adjustment a/c*".

➤ *If there is an increase in the value of assets the :*

Sundry asset a/c   Dr.

To revaluation (**P & L adjustment a/c)**

(This entry will be passed with the increased amount of assets.)

> *If there is decrease in the value of asset the :*
>
> Revaluation **(P/L adjustment)**a/c   **Dr.**
>
>   To sundry assets a/c
>
> (This entry will be passed with decreased amount of assets)

> *If there is provision for doubtful debt or discount reserve etc. on debtor then:*
>
> Revaluation **(P/L adjustment)**a/c   **Dr.**
>
>   To provision for doubtful debt a/c
>
>   To discount reserve on debtor a/c

> *If there an unrecorded asset, Accrued income or prepaid expenses then :*
>
> Sundry asset a/c   **Dr.**
>
> Accrued income a/c   **Dr.**
>
> Prepaid expenses   **Dr.**
>
>   To revaluation (**P & L adjustment a/c**)

> *If there is an increase in amount of liability then :*
>
> Revaluation **(P/L adjustment)**a/c   **Dr.**
>
>   To sundry liabilities a/c
>
> (Note : This entry will be passed with an increased amount of liabilities)

> *If there is an decrease in amount of liability then :*
>
> sundry liabilities a/c   **Dr.**
>
>   To revaluation (**P & L adjustment a/c**)
>
> (This entry will be passed with a decreased amount of Liabilities)

> *If there is any unrecorded amount of liability then :*

Revaluation *(P/L adjustment)*a/c   **Dr.**
            To outstanding exp/liabilities a/c
(This entry will be by passed with amount of outstanding liability)

➢ **When Revaluation a/c is closed then :**

   ✕ **If Profit :**
      Revaluation *(P/L adjustment)*a/c   **Dr.**
               To partner's capital a/c

   ✕ **If loss :**
      Partner's capital a/c   **Dr.**
               To revaluation *(P & L adjustment a/c)*

☐ PRACTICAL SECTION ☐

1. *Charger and Battery are partners of a firm distributing profit or losses of the firm in equal proportion. They decided to change their profit-loss sharing proportion to 2:1 for future. Using the formula of sacrifice made by a partner, calculate what sacrifice has been made by which partner?*

2. *Nokia, Samsung and Akash Tablet are partners of a partnership firm. Profit-loss sharing proportion among them is 5:3:2 All partners decided to change their profit-loss sharing proportion to 2:2:1 Using the formula of sacrifice made by a partner, show the calculation of sacrifice made by partners.*

3. *Nimit, Smit and Yash are partners in a a partnership firm. The proportion of sharing profit-loss among them* **4:4:2.** *On .31/12/01 the balance sheet of their firm is as under.*

Liabilities	Rs.	Assets	Rs.
Capital :		Building	15,00,000
Sab : 7,50,000		Machines	1,50,000
Sony : 7,50,000		Furniture	1,00,000
Star : 3,75,000	18,75,000	Stock	75,000
Creditors	87,500	Debtors	1,00,000
		Bills	
Bills payable	25,000	receivable	25,000
Income received in			
advance	12,500	Bank balance	50,000
	20,00,000		20,00,000

Partners decided to change their profit-loss sharing proportion to **5:3:2** on the date of above balance sheet and decided to revalue assets and liabilities of the business, the information of which is as under :

(1) The value of furniture is to be increased by **Rs. 50,000.**

(2) New value of building is **Rs.14,75,000.**

(3) Market value of machine is calculated **20%** more than its book value.

(4) The value of stock is to be reduced by **Rs. 5,000.**

(5) Provide **5%** bad debts and **7.5%** bad debts reserve on debtors.

(6) Among creditors, **Rs. 5,500** are not to be payable.

(7) Unpaid exp. is **Rs.7,000.**

(8) Outstanding income is **Rs.2,250.**

On the basis of the above information, write journal entries in the books of the firm and prepare Revaluation account.

4. *Colgate and Pepsodent are partners in a partnership firm. The proportion of sharing profit-loss among them 3:2. They decided to change their profit-loss sharing proportion to 2:1 for future. On 31/12/2000, following balances appeared in the books of their firm :*
    1) *Reserve fund (credit balance) – Rs.1,00,000.*
    2) *Workmen profit sharing fund (credit balance) – Rs.35,000.*
    3) *P & L a/c (Debit balance) – Rs.35,000.*
    4) *Workmen accident compensation fund. (credit balance) – Rs.85,000*
    5) *Workmen saving accounts (credit balance) – Rs.1,50,000*

    Pass journal entries showing of accumulated profits and losses in the books of the firm.

5. *Kapil and Sunil are partners sharing profit & loss in 8:6 ratio. Followings are balances as on 31-3-2006 in books of firm.*
    - *Workmen profit sharing fund – Rs.55,000*
    - *P & L A/c (Credit balance) – Rs.10,500*
    - *Reserve fund – Rs.38,500*

- *Workmen accident compensation fund – **Rs.63,000***
- *Depreciation Fund – **Rs.7,000***

Give necessary journal entries in books of firm.

6. *Petrol and Diesel are partners in a partnership firm. The proportion of sharing profit-loss among them **2:1**. They decided to change their profit-loss sharing proportion to **3:2** for future. On .31/12/01 the balance sheet of their firm is as under.*

7. *Pass the journal entry for distribution of accumulated loss at the time of reconstruction of partnership firm.*

*Balance Sheet as on **30/06/2004***

Liabilities	*Rs.*	*Assets*	*Rs.*
Capital :		*Land*	*24,000*
Petrol : 32,000		*Building*	*28,000*
Diesel: 20,000	*52,000*	*Machines*	*8,000*
Current Accounts:		*Furniture*	*4,000*
Petrol : 6,400		*Debtors 5,200*	
Diesel: 5,600	*12,000*	*−B.D.R. 400*	*4,800*
		Receivable	
Profit – loss account	*3,000*	*income*	*4,200*
Creditors	*5,600*	*Bank balance*	*2,000*
Bills payable	*2,400*		
	75,000		*75,000*

Adjustments :

- *The value of Land and Building is to be increased by **15 %** and **10%** respectively.*

- *The value of Furniture and Machines is to be decreased by **15 %** and **10%** respectively.*
- *Total amount of BDR is to be kept at **Rs.500.***
- *Among creditors, **20 %** amount are not to be payable.*
- *Salary of **Rs.1,500** is paid in advance which is not recorded in the books.*
  Write journal entries in the books of the firm and prepare Revaluation account.

🗌 LATEST EXAMINATION 🗌

8. *A,B and C are the partners in the firm . their profit and loss sharing ratio is **5:3:2.** All partners have decided to change profit and loss sharing ratio. The new ratio is **1:1:1.** Calculate the sacrifice ratio of the partners. **(March'09)***

9. *Aan,Ban and Shan are partners of a partnership firm. Profit-loss sharing proportion among them is **4:4:3.** All partners decided to change their profit-loss sharing proportion to **3:3:1** Using the formula of gain received by a partner, show the calculation of gain received by partners. **(March'10)***

10. *Ram, Lakshman and Bharat are partners of a partnership firm. Profit-loss sharing proportion among them is **4:3:3.** All partners decided to change their profit-loss sharing proportion to **3:2:1** Using the formula of gain received by a partner, show the calculation of gain received by partners. **(March'11)***

11. *Priya and Chanda are partners of a firm distributing profit or losses of the firm in equal proportion. They decided to change their profit-loss sharing proportion to **4:1** for future. Mention the calculation for which partner sacrificed and how much? **(March'12)***

12. *Kishor And Manoj are partner sharing profit and loss in a ratio of* **3:2** *on* **31/3/2009** *profit and loss (Debit balance)* **Rs.20,000** *reserve fund* **Rs.15,000** *write down journal entry to distribute this.* **(March'13)**

13. *Kishor, Manoj and Sanjay share profit and loss in equal proportion. They want to change their profit sharing in the ratio of* **5:3:2** *Write partner's gain ratio.* **(March'14)**

............xxxxxxxxx............

CHAPTER – 4
("GOODWILL")

🗒 FORMULAS 🗒

1) *Method of purchase of simple average profits for a certain no. of years:-*

   Average Profit $= \dfrac{\text{Total Profit}}{\text{No. of years}}$

   $\Rightarrow$ Goodwill $=$ Average profit $\times$ Number of year's purchase of Goodwill

2) *Method of purchase of weighted average profits for a certain no. of years:-*

   Weighted Average Profit $= \dfrac{\text{Total weighted Profit}}{\text{Total weight}}$

   $\Rightarrow$ Goodwill = Weighted average profit $\times$ Number of year's purchase of weighted average profit.

🗒 IMPORTANT POINTS 🗒

❖ *When goodwill account is shown/disclosed in the books of a partnership firm – (In Old Ratio)*

❖ *When goodwill account is not shown/disclosed / written off in the books of a partnership firm –*   (**In New Ratio**)

▢ THEORY SECTION ▢

✓ *Definition of Goodwill :*

Goodwill is the value of the reputation of a firm in respect of the profits expected in future over & above the normal profits.

Goodwill is intangible asset.

✓ *Factors Affecting the Value of Goodwill :*

The main factors affecting the value of goodwill are as follows:

1. **Nature of business:** *A firm that produces high value added products orhaving a stable demand is able to earn more profits and therefore has more goodwill.*
2. **Location:** *If the business is centrally located or is at a place having heavy customer traffic, the goodwill tends to be high.*
3. **Efficiency of management:** *A well managed concern usually enjoys theadvantage of high productivity and cost efficiency. This leads to higher profits and so the value of goodwill will also be high.*
4. **Market situation:** *The monopoly condition or limited comp etition enables the concern to earn high profits which leads to higher value of goodwill.*
5. **Special advantages:** *The firm that enjoys special advantag es like importl icences, low rate and assured supply of*

electricity, long-term contracts for supply of materials, well known collaborators, patents, trademarks, etc. enjoy higher value of goodwill.

6. Individual skill and Proficiency : *In some business, success of a business depends on skills or ability of the business owner or owners. In such cases, the value of goodwill of the business is very low as the successful person can't sale his skills.*

(March'09,13)

✓ **Methods of Valuation of Goodwill :-**

So future maintainable profit is significant factor for valuation of Goodwill. There are three methods on the basis of this factor the valuation of goodwill.

× **Method of purchase of simple average profits for a certain no. of years.**

× **Method of purchase of weighted average profits for a certain no. of years.**

× **Capitalization of average profits method.**

× **Method of purchase of super for a certain no. of years.**

a) **Method of purchase of simple average profits for a certain no. of years:-**

Under this method, the average profit of certain year's is to ascertain for valuation of Goodwill. In the second stage, it is to be ascertained that now long this average profit will be maintained, and then *average profit is to be multiplied with those years of purchase. And arrived amount is called as price or value of Goodwill.*

$$\text{Average Profit} = \frac{\text{Total Profit}}{\text{No. of years}}$$

➤ *Goodwill =   Average profit ✗ Number of year's purchase of Goodwill*

b) **Method of purchase of weighted average profits for a certain no. of years:-**

When the profit of last predetermined year's has increasing trend, under such circumstances, per weighted average method, we should give more weight to the profit of recent years and give comparatively less weight to the profits of previous years.

$$\text{Weighted Average Profit} = \frac{\text{Total weighted Profit}}{\text{Total weight}}$$

➤ **Goodwill = Weighted average profit ✗ Number of year's purchase of weighted average profit.**

c) **Capitalization of average profits method:-**

For valuation of goodwill under this method of capitalization of average profit, three important aspects are to be considered :

(1) *Average profit of business (Simple weighted average whichever is applicable),*

(2) *Normal/ expected rate of return of business,*

(3) *Capital employed in the business.*

*Under this method the first step is the determination of average profit and then take up computation of its capitalized value on the basis of normal rate of return. This arrived capitalized value of profit is known as capitalized profit, Thus, Capitalized profit means capitalized value of average profit on the basis of the expended rate of return. If the value of capitalized average profit exceeds the value of capital employed in the business, the difference is designated as " **Goodwill"***

Step : 1 *Average Profit / Weighted Average Profit*

$$= \frac{Total\ Profit\ /\ Total\ weighted\ Profit}{No.\ of\ years/\ Total\ weight}$$

Step : 2 *Capitalized Average Profit* =

$$\frac{Average\ Profit\ /\ weighted\ average\ Profit}{Expected\ rate\ of\ Return}$$

Step : 3 *Capital employed : (Which is given in the sum)*

Step : 4 *Goodwill = Capitalized value of average profit – Capital employed.*

(March'14)

d) **Method of purchase of super for a certain no. of years:-**

The value of goodwill is concerned with additional earning ability of than the average of all firms.

This additional amount of profit is known as super profit. The excess of average profit over normal profit is super profit. The super profit, Thus acquired is multiplied with the number of to determine the value of Goodwill.

During the application of this method, two issue (aspects) are to be considered

(1) Average profit of the business (Simple or weighted whichever is applicable).

(2) Normal or expected profit of the business.

Step : 1   *Average Profit / Weighted Average Profit   = Total Profit / Total weighted Profit*

No. of years/ Total weight

Step : 2   *Normal Expected Return = Capital Employed ✗ Expected Rate of return.*

Step : 3   *Super profit = Average Profit – Normal/ Expected Profit*

Step : 4   *Goodwill = Super profit ✗ The given number of years purchase*

✓ **Accounting Treatment of Goodwill:-**

   i. *When goodwill account is not shown in the books following two heads :*

   ii. *When goodwill account is shown in the books of a partnership firm*

✗**When Goodwill Account is not shown in the Books of a partnership Firm:**

   1) **To Record the Value of Goodwill, The Following Entry will be passed : (In Old Ratio)**

Date	Particulars	Debit	Credit
1/4/2012	Goodwill A/c Dr. To X's capital a/c To Y's capital a/c To Z's capital a/c		

2) When Goodwill will be written off : (In New Ratio)

Date	Particulars	Debit	Credit
1/4/2012	X's capital a/c Dr. Y's capital a/c Dr. Z's capital a/c Dr. To Goodwill a/c		

3) When the Accounting effect of Goodwill is given directly to the partner's capital account without creating Goodwill Account:

Date	Particulars	Debit	Credit
1/4/2012	Partner's capital a/c Dr. (Gained) To Partner's capital a/c (Sacrificed)		

× **When Goodwill Account is shown in the Books of a Partnership Firm :**

i. When new value of goodwill determined is similar to disclosed value of goodwill.

ii. When new value of goodwill determined is more than disclosed value of goodwill.

iii. *When new value of goodwill determined is less than disclosed value of goodwill.*

♣ *When new value of goodwill determined is similar to disclosed value of goodwill.*

- *No entry*

♣ ***When New Value of Goodwill is Determined More than the Disclosed Value of Goodwill :***

- ***When new value of Goodwill is determined more than the disclosed value of Goodwill : (In Old Ratio and Difference between new value of Goodwill and Old value of Goodwill)***

Date	Particulars	Debit	Credit
1/4/2012	Goodwill A/c Dr. To X's capital a/c To Y's capital a/c To Z's capital a/c		

♣ ***When new Value of Goodwill is determined less than disclosed value of Goodwill :***

- ***When new value of Goodwill is determined less than the disclosed value of Goodwill : (In Old Ratio and Difference between old value of Goodwill and new value of Goodwill)***

Date	Particulars	Debit	Credit
1/4/2012	X's capital a/c Dr. Y's capital a/c Dr. Z's capital a/c Dr. To Goodwill a/c		

⬚ PRACTICAL SECTION ⬚

1. *Jitendra, Rashmi and Sapna are partnership firm. Their profit sharing ratio is **2:2:1** The partners have decided to change their profit sharing ratio to **3:2:1** for the future and to make valuation of goodwill. As per partnership agreement, it is decided that the value of goodwill is to be determined for five years purchase of average profit of last 3 years.*

Year	2006	2007	2008	2009	2010
profit (Rs.)	10,000	2,000	5,000	-5,000	15,000

2. *From their following determine weighted average profit :*

Year	2000	2003	2002	2004	2001
profit (Rs.)	7,000	16,000	14,500	24,000	13,000

3. *By using the appropriate average, determine the value of goodwill on the basis of six year's purchase :*

Year	1992	1993	1994	1995	1996
profit(Rs.)	-6,500	-11,000	5,000	8,000	10,000

4. *M, N and P are partners of a firm sharing profit in the ratio of **2:2:1** The value of goodwill is not disclosed in the books of the firm. They have changed their profit sharing ratio to **3:2:1** and decided to have value of goodwill of the firm at*

Rs.84,000 *From the above information, pass necessary journal entries in the books of the partnership firm.*

❖ *When full amount of goodwill is to be shown in the books of firm.*

❖ *When partners do not desire to show goodwill account in the books.*

❖ *Ehen the effect of goodwill is to be given directly to the partners capital account*

(without creating goodwill account)

5. *Gujarati, Hindi and English are partners of a firm sharing profit in the ratio of* **4:3:3** *The value of goodwill of* **Rs. 1,25,000** *is disclosed in the books of the firm. They have changed their profit sharing ratio to* **5:2:3** *and to make revaluation of goodwill. For each of the following, pass necessary journal entries in the books of the partnership firm.*

   i. *When the value of goodwill is increased by* **Rs.35,000.**

   ii. *When the value of goodwill is written off after increase in the value of goodwill as mentioned above in* **(1).**

   iii. *When the value of goodwill is reduced by* **Rs.25,000.**

   iv. *When the value of goodwill is written off after reduction in the value of goodwill as mentioned above in* **(3).**

▢ LATEST EXAMINATION ▢

6. From the following information of a partnership firm, compute the value of goodwill at two years purchase of weighted average profit on the basis of last five years.

Year	2001	2002	2003	2004	2005
profit(Rs.)	10,000	12,000	15,000	18,000	25,000

(March'09)

7. By using the weighted average, determine the value of goodwill on the basis of **3** years' purchase.

Year	2003	2004	2005	2006	2007
profit (Rs.)	25,000	37,500	40,000	50,000	60,000

(March'10)

8. By using the appropriate average, determine the value of goodwill on the basis of **3** years' purchase.

Year	2001	2002	2003	2004	2005
profit(Rs.)	40,000	35,000	32,500	25,000	22,500

(March'11)

9. From the following information of a partnership firm, compute the value of goodwill at five years purchase of weighted average profit on the basis of last five years.

Year	2005	2007	2009	2008	2006
Profit(Rs.)	30,000	45,000	80,000	60,000	40,000

(March'12)

10. From the following information, calculate the value of goodwill, at five years purchase of average profit on the basis of last five years. *(March'13)*

Year	2006	2007	2008	2009
Profit Rs.	40,000	35,000	-15,000	60,000

11. From the following information, calculate the value of goodwill at **4** years, purchase of average profit on the basis of last 5 years : *(March'14)*

Year	2006	2007	2008	2009
Profit Rs.	20,000	-5,000	15000	6,000

.............×××××××××.............

**** _____ *The End* _____ ****

www.ingramcontent.com/pod-product-compliance
Lightning Source LLC
Chambersburg PA
CBHW080832180526
45168CB00006B/2650